You are amazing
and wonderful!
—Psalm 139

♡

Victoria
Nelson

PRAISE FOR
Hiya Moriah

"As a mother of two children who have Down syndrome, I have learned it is imperative to the health and wellbeing of humanity that we do life with people who are different than us and strive for a more inclusive world. *Hiya Moriah* is a powerful tool for just that. It is with the heart of a mother; the passion of an advocate and the grace of a teacher, that Victoria has given us the gift of this book. I hope every parent, educator and human adds it to their library."

–**HEATHER AVIS**, Author of *The Lucky Few*, Speaker, Shouter of Worth

"*Hiya Moriah* is beautifully written and illustrated. It documents the heartwarming journey of one brave child born with special needs, and will serve and as an inspirational, educational, and comforting tool for many."

–**FRANK HANLEY MD**, Executive Director, Betty Irene Moore Children's Heart Center, Lucile Packard Children's Hospital

"Real superheroes live in the hearts of children fighting big battles. Victoria Nelson is a superhero and mother who's beautiful book provides a mean for parents and their children to learn about complex medical conditions. With such understanding, hope, help and love, young and old can provide a brighter future for all children."

–**PHILIPPE S. FRIEDLICH, MD**, Teresa and Byron Pollitt Family Chair in Fetal & Neonatal Medicine, Professor of Pediatrics & Surgery, USC Keck School of Medicine, Director, Fetal and Neonatal Institute, Children's Hospital Los Angeles

"*Hiya Moriah* is a wonderfully written and inspiring children's book about a courageous child. With rhythmic cadence and a rainbow of diverse, brilliant colors, it illustrates how differences can come together and have a penetrating effect on a young reader. Moriah's love of life and engaging personality brings children together. Her physical limitations and the medical equipment she requires, become educational tools to spark curiosity and break down barriers rather than dividing them."

–**DEREK Y. OBAYASHI, MD**, Chair, Department of Pediatric Specialties, Chief, Department of Pediatric Cardiology, Sutter Health / Palo Alto Medical Foundation

"Moriah, the little girl featured in *Hiya Moriah*, is more than a children's book character. She is an ambassador who shows children and adults how to look beyond someone's special needs and disabilities to see the person within. Author Victoria Nelson uses humor and sensitivity to tell Moriah's story from a child's perspective. The illustrations normalize medical and mobility equipment and the text teaches children with and without disabilities to become friends. Hiya Moriah belongs on the shelf of every public, school, and church library so children and adults can read it time and time again."

–JOLENE PHILO, author of the Different Dream Parenting series and *Every Child Welcome: A Ministry Handbook for Including Kids with Special Needs*

"Certain stories inspire us, some entertain us, and others teach us. Hiya Moriah, much like the real life Moriah, does all three. Moriah's story is special, not because she had special needs, but because of who she was as a person. She couldn't speak, but she spoke volumes. She couldn't breathe without a ventilator, but she was herself a breath of fresh air. She couldn't walk, but she ran circles around everyone who knew her. This is a story that will change lives, hearts and minds, just like Moriah. It is a story that needs to be told, and a book that needs to be read."

–DEVON DABBS, Co-founder, Children's Hospice and Palliative Care Coalition

"For all people, but kids in particular, a sense of familiarity with bodies or brains that may work differently from their own is an important part of breaking stigma and becoming open to building relationships. *Hiya Moriah* is especially wonderful in the way it exposes its young readers (and their parents) to some common medical devices in a straightforward and positive way. The diagrams and colorful pictures are especially helpful, as is getting a chance to know about Moriah's equipment but also her favorite activities and personality. Thankful to Victoria Nelson for this book, and for the ways that after reading it kids' hearts and minds may be more open to approaching their peers who use medical equipment and/or have a chronic illness."

–DR. BETHANY MCKINNEY FOX, Director of Access and adjunct professor of Christian ethics at Fuller Theological Seminary, founding pastor of Beloved Everybody Church, and author of Disability and the Way of Jesus: Holistic Healing in the Gospels and the Church (IVP Academic)

"Moriah was an inspirational child who, with the help of her extraordinary parents, rose above the physical limitations imposed by her medical condition. "Hiya Moriah" incorporates the elements of love, understanding, humor, and education to illustrate both the challenges and gifts that having a disability can bring. It reminds us that making friends and being accepted is a very important part of life for all children. This book is a source of inspiration for families facing similar journeys and can be a reminder to all of us that having a disability should not be a barrier to experiencing happiness and rich, beautiful interpersonal connections.

–MANUEL GARCIA, MD, Chief, Division of Pediatric Gastroenterology, Santa Clara Valley Medical Center

"*Hiya Moriah* is an inspirational book depicting a courageous child with special needs. It is rare to see children's books illustrate the journey of kids who have special needs; however, Victoria Nelson does an amazing job sharing this experience. As a mother and a health care provider, I have yet to see other books comparable to this one. This is a long needed gift for families to gain perspective about children with medical conditions and other special needs."

–**JANA NORRIS, PNP**, Pediatric Nurse Practitioner, Cardiac Intensive Care Unit,
   Lucile Packard Children's Hospital

"Victoria and Justin are wonderful followers of Jesus and marvelous parents to their beautiful children. The gift of their precious daughter with special needs, Moriah, took them on an unexpected journey with God and each other. God's love and beauty were revealed to their family in a deep, though painful way. Let Victoria share with you the gift of Moriah's life to us all as only a loving mother can."

–**NICK PALERMO**, Founder of Young Life Capernaum Ministries, Founder and current co-director of
   Emmaus Inn Ministries

"All I can say is 'Yay for *Hiya Moriah*!' You will want to cheer as well when you read this warm invitation to remember that every person is unique and special. Moriah will help you pick up tips and vocabulary for communicating with people whose challenges are different than your own."

–**DAN BAUMGARTNER**, Sr. Pastor, First Presbyterian Church of Hollywood (CA)

"*Hiya Moriah* is a wonderful book. Children are naturally curious, and the book demystifies medical, mobility, and communication equipment that might be used by a classmate with special needs. Engaging and educational, the book encourages interaction and friendships in inclusive settings. A perfect tool for parents, teachers, counselors, school nurses and other school staff."

–**ANN SCHULTE, PHD**, School Psychologist

"I'm all in favour of any publication that spreads information and understanding about CHARGE syndrome, and this book does exactly that in a very accessible and positive way. I always think of Moriah as a force of nature, a personality constantly going out to meet with and confront the world, so it seems entirely appropriate that she should now be the messenger with this important information. I think the glossary of medical terms will be especially helpful and fascinating for young children who are always puzzled and intrigued by things like gastrostomy tubes and trachs. I imagine this book will be a great ambassador for everyone with this complex syndrome."

–**DAVID BROWN**, Deafblind Educational Specialist

Hiya Moriah

Written by Victoria Nelson
Illustrated by Boddz

© 2019 Victoria Nelson

ISBN 978-1-63393-787-1

Published by

An imprint of

◄ köehlerbooks™

210 60th Street
Virginia Beach, VA 23451
800-435-4811
www.koehlerbooks.com

Hiya Moriah

Victoria Nelson

ILLUSTRATED BY **Boddz**

DEDICATION

To my Moriah,

You taught me about love.
Not only how to love you, but to love others.
You showed me how to see beyond the surface,
into the world you brought me.
You taught me that there was so much more
beyond words, beyond looks, beyond what is "normal,"
beyond what is expected.
You showed me how to look into people's eyes,
and see their beauty and worth,
and to love them for who they really are . . .
and for this, I thank you.

To my husband, Justin, who has been my rock since
I was sixteen years old.

To Jadon, Olivia, and Shane, may you remember to be kind,
no matter where you are or who is watching.

I love you from the bottom of my heart.

Hiya! I'm Moriah! I'm seven.

My mama says I'm a gift from Heaven.
God made us special–both you and me.

Plus, I've a few extra things; do you see?
I was born with a syndrome called CHARGE,
which brought challenges–both small and large.

These different challenges taught me to be
super-duper strong, cool, and carefree!

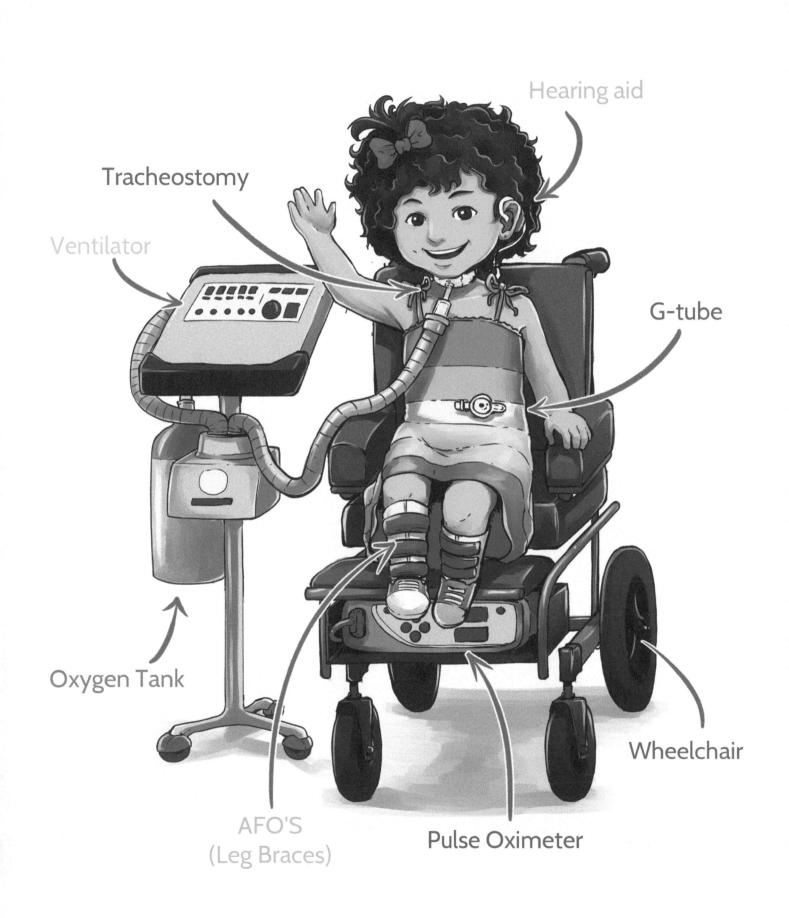

Hearing aid

Tracheostomy

Ventilator

G-tube

Oxygen Tank

Wheelchair

AFO'S
(Leg Braces)

Pulse Oximeter

When I was born, my **heart** was missing a part,
so I had **surgery** right from the start.

I put on a brave face, giving it my best,
and gained a zipper-shaped scar on my chest.

Nurses and doctors helped me get stronger,
but, I stayed in the hospital for a little longer.

Doctors saw that I had trouble with eating
and put a tube in my tummy to help with feeding.

A **gastrostomy tube**, or **g-tube** for short,
helped me get food from a small port.

One thing that I was most happy about?
I didn't taste medicine in my mouth!

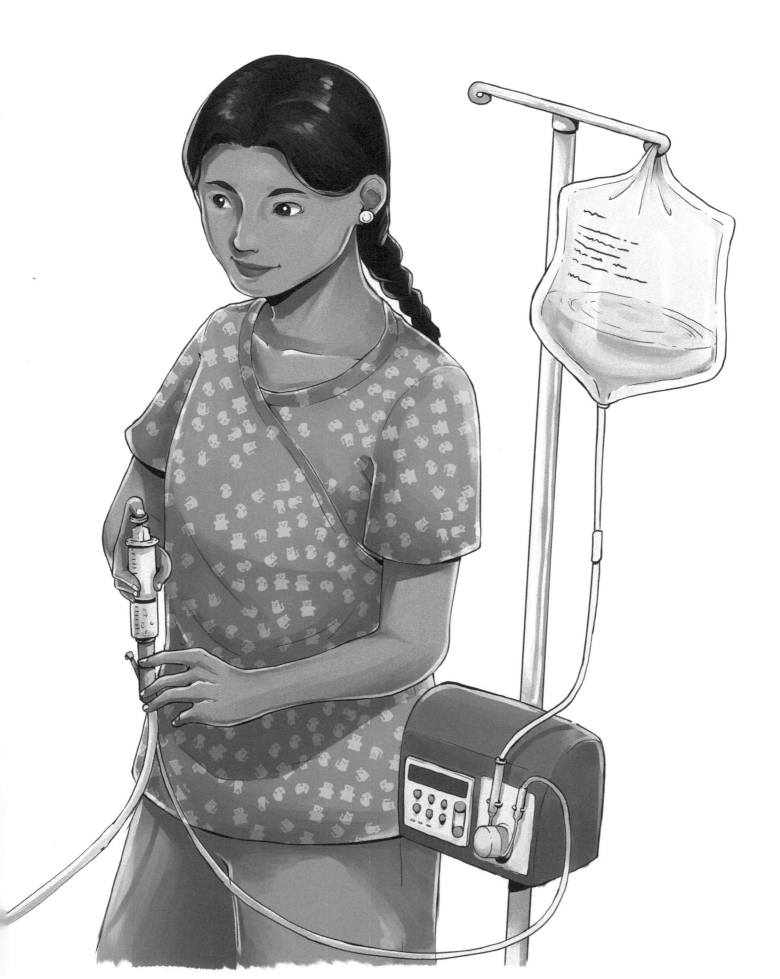

In addition to having
trouble eating,
I needed a little help
with my breathing.

Doctors placed a **tracheostomy**, also known as a trach,
and attached a **ventilator** for my breathing's sake.

The **trach** is in my neck and acts like a nose,
and the **vent** helps my lungs with the air it blows.

The ventilator connects to the trach with a tube
and gives just enough room to dance,
bounce, and move!

I finally go home, and have nurses who help,
but I play around, and make them all yelp!

I wait until their hands are very busy,
then I tickle their arms, and cause a big tizzy.

I giggle and laugh, on the floor I fall,
and because I'm cute, I get away with it all.

Unless Mommy and Daddy catch me on the spot;
I get a "time out," whether I like it or not.

I have many therapies most of my days,
learning to walk and talk in different ways.

A **wheelchair** and **walker** help me get around,
while **leg braces** help me to step up and down.

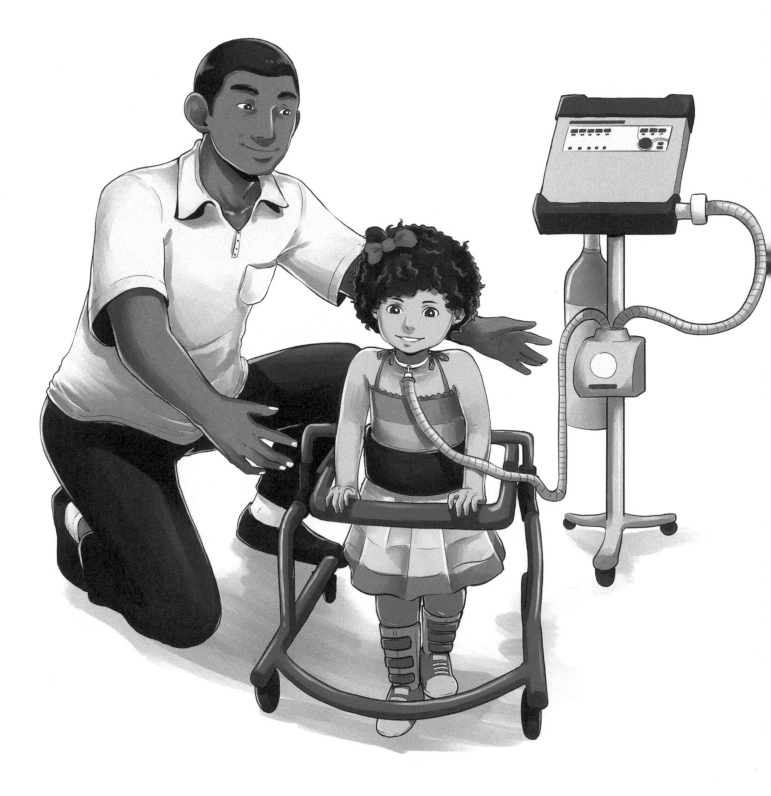

Even with these things, nothing can stop me.
I love to wrestle with my brothers and daddy.

Going to the park can
sometimes be tricky,
but as long as there are
ramps, it's a big victory.

My sister and I love going high on swings,
and imagine we're flying with great, big wings.

Because I have trouble **talking** and hearing,
I speak with my fingers, and children are peering.

My brother and sister have to explain:
Sign language is the name of the game!

In addition to signing, I use **pictures** to show what I want—like books or stickers.

An **ai**d in my ear also helps me to hear,
but shh! At clean-up time, I make it disappear!

I go to school with my nurse
on a **wheelchair-friendly** bus,
but first,
"What bow should you wear?"
my mother will fuss.

At school, my friends come to see me in class.
"What's this? What's that?" the children ask.

My nurse happily answers any question,
but having **clean hands** is her first suggestion.

I can catch a cold a lot easier than most,
and need protection from germs that are gross.

After scrubbing and washing the dirt off their hands,
the kids push my wheelchair wherever I command.

We **laugh** and **play**, and they call me Thumbelina
because I'm the size of a tiny ballerina.

The thing about me that you really should know:
I love to make friends wherever I go.

I might seem different in the very beginning,
but, as soon as we play, it sends our hearts spinning.

So, next time you see someone like me, Moriah,
you can introduce yourself; just wave, and say, "Hiya."

You're showing you care about someone who's new, and you might even make a new friend or two!

This new friend can teach you to see

the person on the **inside**–like my friends taught me.

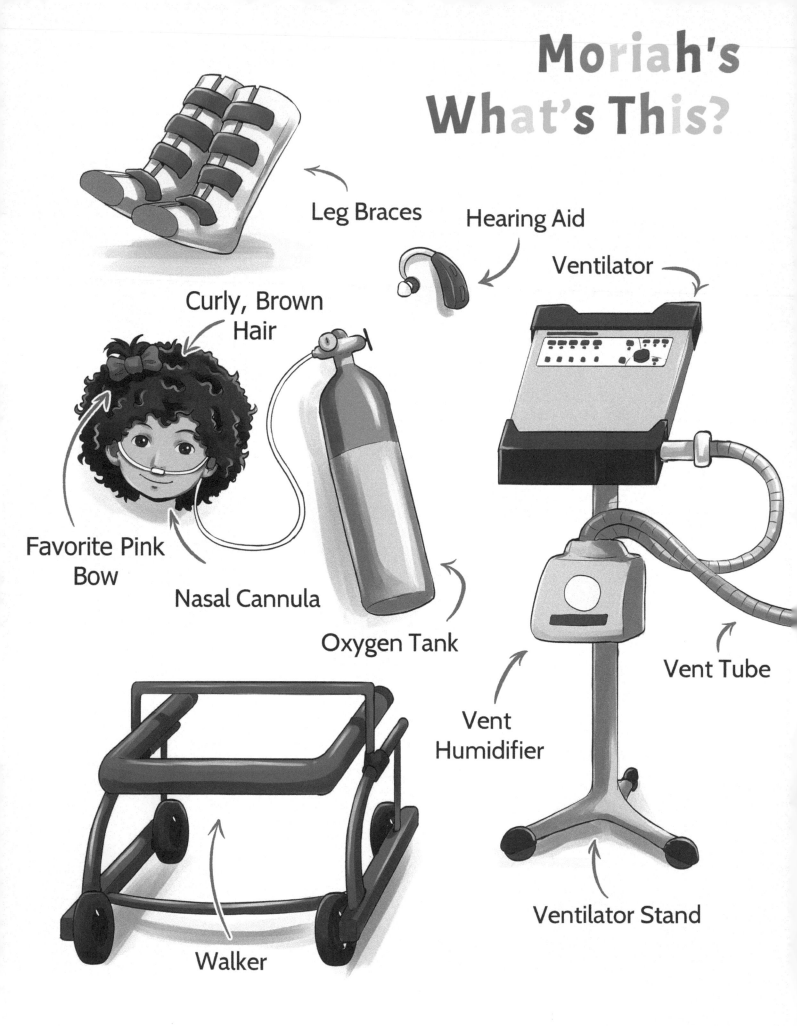

Moriah's What's This?

Leg Braces

Hearing Aid

Ventilator

Curly, Brown Hair

Favorite Pink Bow

Nasal Cannula

Oxygen Tank

Vent Tube

Vent Humidifier

Ventilator Stand

Walker

What's That?

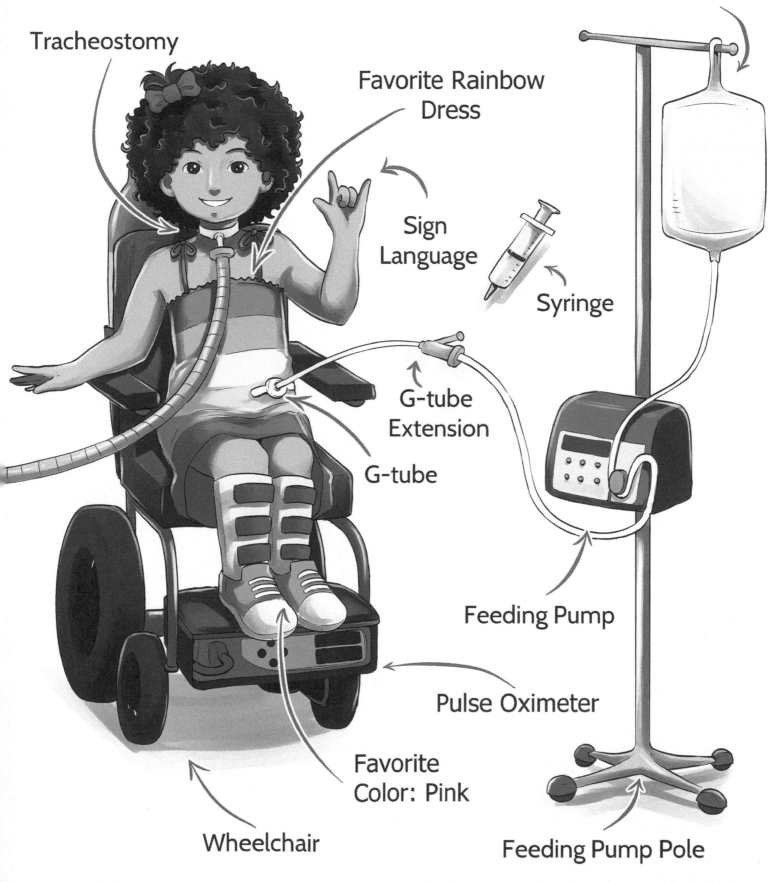

Tracheostomy

Favorite Rainbow Dress

Feeding Bag

Sign Language

Syringe

G-tube Extension

G-tube

Feeding Pump

Pulse Oximeter

Favorite Color: Pink

Wheelchair

Feeding Pump Pole

What's This?

CHARGE Syndrome
I was born with CHARGE Syndrome, which affects different areas of my body, including vision, heart, breathing, growth, balance, and hearing. All of my friends with CHARGE are unique, and we usually impress everyone around us with how much we can overcome!
To learn more about CHARGE, please visit chargesyndrome.org

Gastrostomy Tube, also known as a g-tube
A tube that goes in my stomach to help me get food, since I don't eat much by mouth. I'm going to therapy to learn how to eat, but in the meantime, I have what looks like a cute little button in my stomach

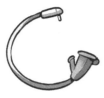

G-tube Extension
A long tube that connects to my g-tube.
The end of the tube has a little opening with a cap, called a port, and this is where a syringe or feeding bag connects. The port can be closed when we're not using it, but you have to be careful because sometimes it accidentally opens, and food can spill everywhere!

Feeding or Medicine Syringe
A small, plastic tube in the shape of a cylinder that can be used to give formula, medicine, or even blended food. A plunger is used to push the formula or medicine through the syringe. The syringe goes into the port of my g-tube extension.

Feeding Bag, Feeding Pump, and Feeding Pump Pole
A feeding pump is a machine that pumps formula into my g-tube. We pour forumla into the feeding bag, hook the feeding bag into the machine, and it pumps away! The feeding bag and pump hang from a feeding pole. I usually use the feeding pole at night, but during the day when I'm on the go, I use a special backpack that holds the feeding bag and feeding pump.

Hearing Aid
A device that I wear in my ear to make sound louder since I can't hear very well.

Sign Language
A language that doesn't use words, but uses hand gestures to communicate. I use sign language because I am hard of hearing, and this is my way of talking to you. This sign means "I love you."

Leg brace, also known as AFO (Ankle Foot Orthosis)
A brace, in the shape of an L, that I use to support my legs.

What's That?

Walker
A metal frame with wheels that helps me when I'm walking.

Wheelchair
A chair with wheels that I use to get around, since I can't totally walk on my own. A Wheelchair can be pushed or it can be electric, powered by a motor. I wish I had an electric wheelchair, but my mom won't let me get one. If I had it, I'd go super fast on the playground!

Congenital Heart Defect or CHD
CHD is when a part of the heart might be missing, or a part might be in the wrong place, and surgery may be needed to fix it. I was born with a heart defect, and I've had several heart surgeries. Now, the scar on my chest from surgery looks like a cool zipper.

Nasal Cannula
A tube that connects to an oxygen tank, and delivers oxygen into my nose. Since I have trouble breathing, I need a little more oxygen than others. But ever since I got my tracheostomy, I don't need to wear a nasal cannula on my face anymore; the oxygen can connect to my ventilator and tracheostomy tube.

Oxygen Tank
A metal, cylinder-shaped storage container that holds oxygen. Everyone needs oxygen to breathe, but some people need extra when they have trouble breathing.

Pulse Oximeter
A machine that measures my oxygen level and heart rate. It has a sensor that can be wrapped around my finger or toe to measure it.

Tracheostomy, also known as a Trach
A tracheostomy is the hole in my neck, which was made so that I have another air way to breathe from. It can be placed when a pearson has a really hard time breathing. A trach tube is placed in the hole, and is held in place with a trach tie.

Ventilator, also known as a Vent
A machine that gives me breaths, and supports my lungs since I can't breathe on my own. It connects to my trach with a long, blue tube that gives me enough room to move around.

Ventilator Stand
A stand that holds my ventilator. My ventilator can also go on my wheelchair in a ventilator backpack whenever I go out.

Since we are each unique in many a way,
make your own "What's This? What's That?"
for you to display!

ACKNOWLEDGMENTS

With special gratitude to all the nurses, doctors, therapists, teachers, and anyone else who is making a difference in the lives of children with medical and special needs.

Your care and devotion to helping our kids is beyond measure. We, as parents, appreciate the grace and patience given to us as we learn to navigate this new normal with our children. Your family-centered care will help make our child's foundation strong and cohesive. The more we can do to give our children a thriving foundation, the more our children will shine like the stars that they are.

Moms and Dads,
You have this, and I'm cheering you on.

"I praise you because you made me in
an amazing and wonderful way.
What you have done is wonderful
I know this very well."
Psalm 139:14

CPSIA information can be obtained
at www.ICGtesting.com
Printed in the USA
BVHW021337200319
543152BV00001B/6/P